Unit 1 · Europe in 1945

Source 1

American and Soviet soldiers on the Elbe, April 1945. The American is the one on the left with a rifle on his back.

On 27 April 1945 American and Soviet troops met beside the River Elbe in northern Germany. Three days later, Adolf Hitler, the Nazi dictator, committed suicide in Berlin. On 8 May Germany surrendered unconditionally to the Allies.

The men pictured in Source 1 who had helped to defeat Germany did not belong to Europe. Home for the Americans was thousands of miles away to the west, across the Atlantic, and the greater part of the Soviet Union was in Asia, not Europe. Their countries, the United States and the Soviet Union, towered over the rest of the world because of the size of their populations and the strength of their military forces. They could accurately be described as 'superpowers' and would dominate the world for the next 40 years. Somehow, in a new and very different world, caught between these superpowers, a broken and exhausted Europe had to reshape itself.

The meeting of American and Soviet soldiers on the banks of the Elbe in 1945 marked the end of an era in both European and world history. For 400 years the nations of Europe had dominated the world. That age was now over and they themselves had speeded its end by letting loose two world wars between 1914 and 1945. The rest of this Unit shows how, as a result of these wars, Europe in 1945 had to start adapting to a new era in world history.

1945: The start of a new era

The effects of the Second World War

The problems which Europe faced were enormous. In April 1945, Konrad Adenauer returned to Cologne in Germany where in the 1930s he had been Oberburgermeister (Mayor) before being dismissed and later imprisoned by the Nazis. He was appalled by what he found:

Source 2

Konrad Adenauer, *Memoirs 1945–53*, 1965.

The city's population before the war had been roughly 760,000. Now there were about 32,000 . . .. More than half of the houses and public buildings were totally destroyed, nearly all the others had suffered partial damage . . ..There was no gas, no water, no electric current and no means of transport . . .. The bridges across the Rhine had been destroyed. There were mountains of rubble in the streets . . .. People were living as best they could in the cellars of bombed houses. They did their cooking on primitive brick fireplaces . . .. They fetched water in pails and tin bowls from the few pumps that had remained intact . . ..

Such scenes could be found all over Europe. The Second World War was even more ferocious than the First World War and was fought with a greater contempt for human life. Civilians were victims as much as soldiers, as bombing by plane and rocket caused destruction on an unprecedented scale. Central and Eastern Europe suffered the most. The Soviet Union may have lost as many as 27 million people, Poland 4.3 million and Germany 4.2 million. To these dreadful figures must be added the 6 million Jews murdered by the Nazis. Though Western European nations such as Britain and France suffered fewer military casualties than in the First World War, their ports and industrial cities were far more badly damaged. Source 3 shows some of the effects on the Netherlands of the retreat of the occupying German forces in the last months of the war.

Source 3

The Netherlands under water in 1945, after the dykes which held back the sea had been broken in the fighting.

The economic damage was colossal. Mines and factories were ruined; road and railway systems dislocated; crops flattened and orchards destroyed. In 1946 the industrial production of Europe was only a third of the 1938 figure and the continent could not feed itself. The French calculated that the war had cost them more than 40 per cent of their total wealth. There was also great psychological damage. Governments and those peoples they governed saw the damage around them and feared that it would take a generation or more to repair it.

American capitalism and Soviet communism

Almost at once, Europe found itself caught between the two superpowers, the United States to the west and the Soviet Union to the east. These had nothing in common except their victory over the Nazis.

The United States was a democracy, with a President elected every four years. Much the richest country in the world, it was also technologically and industrially the most advanced. The Americans believed in capitalism, which encouraged the private ownership of business, free trade and governments interfering as little as possible in people's lives. They believed success was due to their capitalist democracy and free enterprise.

In contrast, the Soviet Union was run by members of the Communist Party headed by an all-powerful dictator, Joseph Stalin. Communism taught that capitalism was evil, since in a capitalist society the few rich, by their control of a nation's wealth, got richer at the expense of the many workers who were bound to remain poor. In a communist state, everyone was in theory supposed to work for the common good. The means of production such as mines, factories and railways were publicly, not privately owned. This enabled the government to use the nation's wealth to benefit everyone, not just the rich. The Soviet government interfered much more than the American government in the lives of its citizens, strictly controlling many aspects of life, such as newspapers, education, painting and music.

The division of Europe and the 'Cold War'

The two sides viewed each other with fear and distrust. Winston Churchill, the British Prime Minister, had made the 'Western' position very clear in his much-quoted 'iron curtain' speech in 1946:

Source 4

Winston Churchill, from a speech at Fulton, Missouri, USA, 5 March 1946.

From Stettin on the Baltic to Trieste on the Adriatic, an iron curtain has descended across the continent. Behind that line lie all the capitals of the ancient states of central and eastern Europe . . . all these famous cities and the populations around them lie in the Soviet sphere and all are subject . . . to a very high and increasing measure of control from Moscow . . ..

I do not believe that Soviet Russia desires war. What they desire are the fruits of war and the indefinite expansion of their power and doctrines. I am convinced that there is nothing which they admire as much as strength and there is nothing for which they have less respect than military weakness.

Source 5

Europe in 1949.

Source 5

Europe in 1949.

Key

- Communist states dominated by the USSR
- Other communist states
- European states in NATO
- Divided cities
- the Iron Curtain
- Post-war boundary of USSR
- Pre-war boundary of USSR

A week later, Stalin made the Soviet position equally clear in an interview published by the newspaper *Pravda*:

Source 6

Joseph Stalin, *Pravda*, 13 March 1946.

Mr Churchill now takes the stand of the warmongers and in this Mr Churchill is not alone. He has friends not only in Britain but in the United States of America as well . . . Mr Churchill sets out to unleash war with a race theory, asserting that only English-speaking nations are superior nations, who are called upon to decide the destinies of the entire world.

By 1949 it became clear that the Iron Curtain was not going to rise for many years. Europe was now split in two, with Western Europe closely allied to the United States and Eastern Europe to the Soviet Union. Each side had its military forces on continual alert, believing that the other would attack if it showed the slightest weakness. A grim barrier of barbed wire, mine-fields and heavily guarded frontier posts ran across the continent from north to south. In fact the situation came very close to a war which never quite turned into fighting. This 'Cold War', as it became known, was to last 40 years.

Source 7

This French anti-Soviet cartoon shows Stalin threatening France.

The end of European empires

One other major change marked the end of European world domination; the break-up of European empires overseas. During the 19th century nations such as Britain and France had turned huge areas of Asia and Africa into colonies. They used them mainly for their own benefit and usually controlled them with European officials. The Second World War badly weakened European colonial rule, especially in Asia. The Japanese, an Asian power, heavily defeated British forces at Singapore and occupied the British, Dutch and French colonies in the Far East, before being defeated themselves by the Americans. As a result, resistance to European rule, growing between the wars, grew stronger still after 1945.

The Soviet Union and the United States both strongly opposed European empire-building. The Soviet Union opposed it because it believed this to be the method used by capitalist governments to expand their power all over the world. The USA opposed it because the European rulers refused to allow people in the colonies to govern themselves. In 1941 President Franklin D. Roosevelt for the United States and Churchill for Britain had signed the Atlantic Charter, which set out the principles upon which they planned to act for the good of the world after the defeat of Germany and Japan. The third point of the Charter reads as follows:

Source 8

The Atlantic Charter, 14 August 1941, signed on a warship off the coast of Newfoundland.

They [the USA and Britain] respect the right of all peoples to choose the form of government under which they live; and they wish to see . . . self-government restored to those who have been forcibly deprived of it.

For Roosevelt and his successors in the USA, this meant what it said: all peoples of the world should have the kind of government they wanted, not just those in Europe who had suffered at the hands of the Nazis. So, however much Churchill and other European leaders wished to keep their empires, the forces working against them were too strong. India, much the most important part of the British Empire, won its independence in 1947 and in the same year Indonesia shook off Dutch rule. By 1950 most of Asia was free from European rule and by 1965 most of Africa.

Questions

1 Explain briefly what Sources 2 and 3 tell you about the economic situation in Europe at the end of the war.

2 Britain and France were victorious in 1945. What state were they in at the end of the war?

3 In 1946, what did: a) Churchill believe to be the aims of the USSR; b) Stalin believe to be the aims of Britain and the USA?

4 Explain the terms 'superpower', 'iron curtain' and 'cold war'.

5 Explain in a paragraph how the Second World War changed the balance of power in the world and, in particular, its effects on Europe.

Unit 2 · The Cold War, 1945–1972

Source 1

The Big Three at Yalta: Churchill on the left; Roosevelt, mortally ill, in the centre; and Stalin on the right.

There were many differences between the United States and the Soviet Union but they had fought together against the Nazis and achieved a tremendous victory. When the 'Big Three' met at Yalta in 1945 (Source 1) they disagreed about important points, but believed that they could keep on working together. Certainly Harry Hopkins, Roosevelt's adviser thought Yalta to be:

Source 2

R. E. Sherwood, *Roosevelt and Hopkins: An Intimate History,* 1948.

. . . the dawn of a new day. The Russians had proved that they could be reasonable and there wasn't any doubt in the minds of the President or any of us that . . . we could get along with them peacefully as far into the future as any of us could imagine.

With the war against Germany finally won, another conference took place in the summer of 1945, at Potsdam, near Berlin. As a result of the Yalta and Potsdam conferences broad agreement was reached on the post-war frontiers of Europe.

However, three years later the Iron Curtain had fallen and during the Berlin airlift of 1948–49 (see pages 12–15) a third world war seemed very close. Why did the wartime Allies so quickly become deadly enemies and how did this lead to a division of Europe?

2.1 Towards the Cold War: Eastern Europe 1945–1948

Source 3

Central and Eastern Europe in 1945.

Key
- Land taken by USSR in 1945
- Land taken by Poland in 1945
- Poland 1921–1938
- Polish frontier after 1945

The communist 'take-over' of Eastern Europe

An important cause of the Cold War was the Soviet take-over of Eastern Europe. The Western powers, while happy to have governments in Eastern Europe friendly towards the Soviet Union, wished them to be freely elected. Stalin, however, had different plans. To prevent another German attack (Germany after all had invaded Russia in 1914 as well as in 1941), he wanted a buffer of states between Germany and the USSR, all with communist governments which he could trust. By 1948 he had nearly succeeded in creating these buffer states.

Though events varied from one country to the next, there was a pattern to the communist take-over of Eastern Europe. After the war coalition governments (made up of a number of political parties, communist and non-communist) took office. In these governments Communists held key ministries such as the ministry of the interior (which controlled the police) or of defence (which controlled the army). With the help of the Red (Soviet) Army which had liberated the country but was still in occupation, the Communists turned on the non-communist parties. Using a mixture of terror and vote-rigging, they won large majorities in new elections. Individuals loyal to Stalin led these communist governments and they strengthened their own positions by purges against their opponents.

Poland

For example, in Poland Stalin had set up a communist provisional government in 1944. Roosevelt and Churchill persuaded him that some politicians led by Mikolajczyk (who had set up a Polish government-in-exile during the war in London) should join the provisional government. Though most Poles were strongly anti-Soviet, the Communists won a landslide victory in elections in 1947. This was hardly surprising, since many of Mikolajczyk's Peasant Party workers were imprisoned and their candidates prevented from standing for election. Mikolajczyk, rightly fearing for his life, fled the country. Bierut, the communist chief who had spent the war in Moscow, became leader of a one-party communist state.

By 1948 one-party communist governments also controlled Bulgaria, Romania, Hungary and Czechoslovakia.

Yugoslavia

The only serious setback to Stalin's plans took place in Yugoslavia. There Marshal Tito had liberated his country with little help from the Red Army and, though a Communist, would not take orders from Stalin. 'The Yugoslav brand of communism,' he once said, 'had its origins in the hills and forests and was not imported ready-made from Moscow.' In his own way, Tito was as ruthless as Stalin. He drove the Yugoslav king into exile and had some of his main political rivals killed. In rigged elections in 1945 he won 90 per cent of the seats and became a dictator. At first Stalin strongly supported Tito, but turned against him when Yugoslavia refused to support Soviet plans for the economic development of Eastern Europe. First Stalin tried but failed to overthrow Tito, then he broke off trade links. The Yugoslav economy suffered badly, but Tito managed to forge new trading links with the West and survived.

Source 4

The Soviet Union's actions in Eastern Europe, as seen by the British cartoonist, Low. The caption reads: 'See for yourself. Is it not obvious that they are "democratic governments which enjoy the confidence of the overwhelming majority of the people of these countries?'

SEE FOR YOURSELF.   IS IT NOT OBVIOUS THAT THEY ARE "DEMOCRATIC GOVERNMENTS WHICH ENJOY THE CONFIDENCE OF THE OVERWHELMING MAJORITY OF THE PEOPLE OF THESE COUNTRIES" ?

Questions

1   Study Source 3 and answer these questions:

   a) What lands did the Soviet Union add to its territories?
   b) What lands did Germany lose?
   c) What were the effects of these changes on Poland?
   d) How were Germany and Austria divided and what happened to their capital cities?

2   a) Why did Stalin wish to bring Eastern Europe under the control of Moscow?
   b) How did Stalin bring about the communist 'take-over' of Europe between 1945 and 1949?

3   Who successfully defied Stalin? Why do you think he was successful where other Eastern European leaders failed?

2.2   Towards the Cold War: US attitudes 1946–1947

These events in Eastern Europe caused the United States to move away from the friendly attitudes of Roosevelt and Hopkins (see Source 2). Roosevelt's successor, President Harry S. Truman, was greatly influenced by George C. Kennan, who had been chief adviser to the US Ambassador in Moscow during the war. Kennan believed that the only sensible policy for the USA was to surround the Soviet Union with a ring of strong defensive alliances and to stop it expanding, by force if necessary. As he wrote in 1947:

Source 5

George C. Kennan, writing as 'Mr X' in the magazine *Foreign Affairs*, 1947.

The United States must continue to regard the Soviet Union as a rival, not a partner . . . .

Soviet policies will reflect no love of . . . peace . . . but rather a cautious, persistent pressure towards the disruption and the weakening of all rival influences and rival power.

Kennan and others may have exaggerated Stalin's suspiciousness. They may also have failed to take sufficient note of Soviet concerns about the danger of a revived Germany which Stalin had expressed very clearly in 1946 in his response to Churchill's 'iron curtain' speech:

Source 6

Stalin, interviewed in *Pravda*, 13 March 1946.

The Soviet Union's loss of life [as a result of the German invasion of 1941] has been several times greater than that of Britain and the United States of America put together . . . .

So what can there be surprising about the fact that the Soviet Union, anxious for its future safety, is trying to see to it that governments loyal in their attitude to the Soviet Union should exist in these countries [between Germany and the USSR]?

The Truman Doctrine, 1947

Nevertheless, Truman decided on a tough policy of 'containing' the Soviet Union within its areas or 'spheres' of influence. At Yalta, the Big Three had agreed that Greece should be a British sphere of influence, but a civil war had broken out there between Communists and anti-communists. When, in 1947, the British government said that it could no longer afford to support the anti-communists, Truman decided that the USA must step into Britain's shoes. If the Communists succeeded in Greece, which country would fall to them next? Turkey? Italy? France? In March 1947 he persuaded Congress (the American parliament) to provide military aid to both Greece and Turkey. He argued that Soviet attempts to expand communism were forcing every nation in the world to choose between two ways of life; the Western one, based on majority governments freely elected, or, the Soviet one, where a communist minority fixed elections and used fear to rule the majority. The USA must now act, he declared, on behalf of the free nations of the world:

Source 7

President Truman speaking to Congress, 12 March 1947.

It must be the policy of the United States to support free peoples who are resisting attempted subjugation [having a government forced upon them] by armed minorities or by outside pressures.

Source 8

This American cartoon shows Stalin choking on the Truman Doctrine.

From then on, the USA was ready to use force, if necessary, in those parts of the world where they believed communism seemed likely to expand.

The Marshall Plan, 1947

The next American step, however, was an economic one; the Marshall Plan. George C. Marshall was the American Secretary of State (or Foreign Minister) and three months after Truman's speech (Source 7) he announced a vast scheme of economic aid for Europe. It was in many ways extremely generous:

Source 9

George C. Marshall, speech at Harvard University, 5 June 1947.

Our policy is directed not against any country or doctrine but against hunger, poverty, desperation and chaos.

Eventually $23 billion was spent on Europe through the Plan and it was offered to all Europe, to the East as well as the West. The Soviet leaders looked at the offer closely before rejecting it as too threatening to their own economy and to their control of Eastern Europe. When Czechoslovak leaders continued to show interest in the Plan, they were summoned to Moscow and ordered to ignore it.

The Soviet leaders were not just being bloody-minded. The Plan was more than simply an act of American charity. One of the purposes of the Plan, Marshall made clear, was to bring about an economic recovery in Europe which would help free institutions (including privately owned businesses), to survive.

The Americans were worried that the severe economic problems facing France and Italy were encouraging the growth of communism. The attraction of communism would decrease as Europe's prosperity grew and this would also profit American businesses.

The economy of Eastern Europe was extremely weak and the Soviets feared that their industry, badly damaged during the war, would not be able to compete with American firms. Already Molotov had explained Soviet fears:

Source 10

V. M. Molotov speaking at the Paris Peace Conference, 10 October 1946.

If American capital was given a free hand in the small states ruined . . . by the war . . . [it] would buy up the local industries, appropriate [take possession of] the more attractive . . . enterprises, and would become the master in these small states . . ..

The Soviet leaders denounced the Marshall Plan as part of an American plot to take economic and political control of Europe.

Source 11

This German poster depicts the Marshall Plan as a powerful international lorry (note the many flags) bringing recovery to Europe along the Free Way (Freie Bahn).

Freie Bahn

ZOLL GRENZE

DEM
MARSHALLPLAN

Questions

1   What in Source 6 does Stalin give as his main reason for Soviet policy in Eastern Europe?

2   What Soviet actions caused Truman to announce his Doctrine?

3   What were: a) the economic; b) the political reasons for the Marshall Plan?

4   What did the Soviet leaders think of the Marshall Plan? How reasonable do you think they were being?

Unit 3 · Germany, 1945–1949

The Cold War division of Europe after 1945 was deepest and most dangerous in Germany.

Source 1

Germany, 1945–1949.

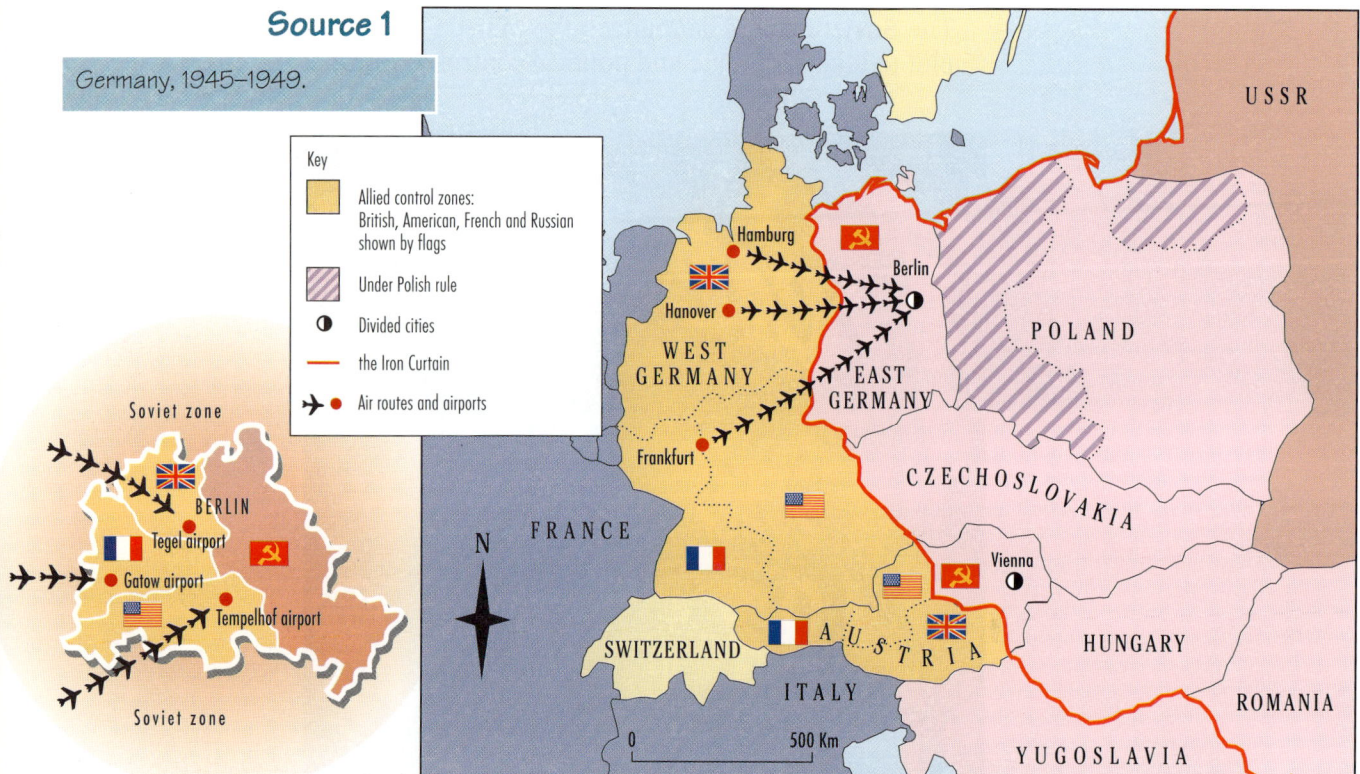

Key

- Allied control zones: British, American, French and Russian shown by flags
- Under Polish rule
- Divided cities
- the Iron Curtain
- Air routes and airports

3.1 Why was the Cold War coldest in Germany?

The Allies and post-war Germany

In 1945 the victorious Allies had agreed that Germany should stay a single country. Though divided into four zones (American, British, French and Soviet), it would be run by a joint Allied Control Commission. Berlin, the capital, though well inside the Soviet zone, was also divided into four zones, to be run by a joint Allied *Kommandatura*, as it became known. When eventually the surviving Nazis had been thoroughly purged, the Allies expected that a democratically elected and disarmed German government would take over from the Commission and *Kommandatura*.

They also agreed that the border between Germany and Poland should be the Oder-Neisse line, well to the west of the 1939 frontiers (see Source 5, page 4) and that the Soviet Union should receive 10 billion dollars' worth of reparations from Germany. To these reparations would be added industrial equipment shifted to the Soviet Union from the British, French and American zones.

Disagreements start

Soon the Allies began to quarrel both within the Commission and the *Kommandatura*. While the Soviet Union and France wanted to keep the Germans economically weak, the United States and Britain believed that it would be best for Europe as well as Germany if the shattered German economy could be restored as quickly as possible. The measures they put into effect to bring about economic recovery, particularly monetary reform, upset the Soviets, who also believed that the West was not honouring the agreement about reparations. In the opinion of the Soviet government, the actions of the West were very threatening:

Source 2

A. A. Gromyko and B. N. Ponomarev (eds), *Soviet Foreign Policy Vol. II*, 1981.

> The Western powers wanted a separate monetary reform as part of their policy of dividing Germany and installing a reactionary [backward-looking] regime hostile to the Soviet Union in West Germany.

For their part, the Western Allies were far from happy with Soviet actions in Berlin. Using methods that were proving so successful in other parts of Eastern Europe, Soviet officials tried to force the unpopular communist and popular socialist parties in Berlin to merge. Their aim was to create a single party loyal to Moscow that would bring the whole of Berlin under Soviet control. The Berlin socialists (SPD), led by Ernst Reuter and Louise Schroder, refused to bow to communist pressure. On 18 March, 1948 Reuter addressed a large demonstration in Berlin:

Source 3

W. Phillips Davison, *The Berlin Blockade*, 1958.

> He pointed out that Prague [the capital of Czechoslovakia] had been overrun by the Communists and Finland was being threatened. 'But,' he added, 'if one should ask who will be next, we can answer firmly and confidently: it will never be Berlin.'

The Berlin Crisis, 1948–1949

Reuter and his colleagues looked to the West for support and soon the situation in Berlin took the world to the brink of a third world war. The crisis built up in stages. First, the Soviets began sometimes to stop vehicles, trains and barges approaching Berlin from the West. Then in March their representative walked out of the Allied Control Commission in protest against Western plans for reforming the currency in their zones. Westerners travelling to Berlin then faced more difficulties; for example, a Soviet fighter shadowing a British transport plane collided with it, killing sixteen people. Britain and the United States, now fully supported by France, continued with their currency reforms. In May 1948, in retaliation, Stalin ordered his representative on the Allied *Kommandatura* in Berlin to walk out and cut all the surface links between the capital and the West. The Soviets placed all the blame on the West:

Source 4

A. A. Gromyko and B. N. Ponomarev (eds), *Soviet Foreign Policy Vol. II*, 1981.

> The unlawful monetary reform . . . threatens to disorganise the whole Soviet zone . . . . The Soviet military authorities find themselves compelled to tighten control of the movement of people and goods between the Eastern and Western zones, including Berlin.

Source 5

American planes queueing to take off at Tempelhof in July 1948 during the airlift. At this stage the airlift continued 24 hours a day.

Stalin's aims were clear. He wanted the Western Allies out of Berlin. Obviously the agreements made in 1945 were not working. To Stalin, the Truman Doctrine and Marshall Plan proved that the West was actively anti-communist. So why should the Westerners stay in Berlin, which had been conquered in 1945 by the Red Army alone? He thought that it would not be difficult to get rid of them. An easily organised blockade would soon starve West Berlin into surrender. Such a setback might also cause the USA to postpone its scheme for uniting West Germany and to co-operate more with the Soviet Union.

The airlift

Stalin miscalculated badly. He underestimated both the airpower of the Western Allies and their readiness to use it. President Truman and General Clay, commander of the United States Army in Europe, saw the blockade of Berlin, which followed soon after the Soviet take-over of Eastern Europe, as another dangerous Soviet bid for the control of Europe. If West Berlin fell, West Germany would surely be the next target. The British government agreed with Truman, so the USA and Britain began to airlift vital supplies to Berlin and made clear to the Soviet Union that attacks on these flights would be treated as a declaration of war.

The airlift lasted eleven months and was a nerve-wracking time. Could West Berlin be saved from starvation? Would the Soviets try to shoot the planes down?

During the winter of 1948–1949 American and British planes provided Berlin with 2.3 million tonnes of supplies. Everything needed for survival was flown in, including 5,000 tonnes of coal per day. It was an astonishing achievement; one day alone saw 1,400 flights. It was also dangerous – 79 Americans, Britons and Germans died in accidents. It was also expensive; costing in all more than $100,000,000.

Source 6

Approach to Tempelhof is the title of this striking painting by American artist Bob Lavin. Tempelhof was the main airport in the American sector of Berlin.

Inside Berlin

As well as near-famine conditions, Berliners suffered tremendous pressure from the Soviets to become part of a single city under a communist government. Anti–communist politicians such as Reuter and Friedensburg had to guard continuously against being overthrown by a Soviet-organised plot. Despite everything, West Berliners were in no doubt whom they supported. When asked in a public opinion poll in July 1948 'Do you believe that the Western powers are right to stay in Berlin?', 98 per cent answered 'Yes', 1 per cent 'No' and 1 per cent were undecided.

The city council openly criticised the Soviet blockade and moved to West Berlin. Many students and teachers from Berlin University (which was in the Soviet zone) also moved to West Berlin, setting up the new Free University. People moved in their thousands from the Soviet zone into West Berlin and from there to West Germany.

It was probably the resistance of the Berliners and the bad impression the blockade gave both to European and international opinion which caused Stalin to call off the blockade in May 1949.

The results of the Berlin blockade

The blockade had many results. It ended the attempts of the victorious Allies of 1945 to work together governing Germany as a single country. The Iron Curtain now cut off the Soviet zone from the rest of Germany and East from West Berlin. The three Western zones came together in 1949 as the Federal Republic of Germany (West Germany) with the Christian Democrat, Konrad Adenauer, as its first Chancellor. It was strongly anti-communist and remained closely allied to the West until the reunification of Germany in 1990. Also in 1949, the Soviet zone became the German Democratic Republic (East Germany) with Otto Grotewohl as its first Prime Minister. It was another Soviet satellite in Eastern Europe, a one-party communist state closely bound to Moscow.

More than any other single event, the Berlin blockade made it clear to the world that the Cold War existed. The two superpowers now had Europe divided between them. They believed themselves to be enemies and each was determined to prevent the other gaining any more power.

The blockade also showed that the Cold War was not a hot war. The airlift brought both sides close to war but each took great care to avoid fighting. So they continued until the 1980s, arming and re-arming, criticising and threatening, but never actually going to war against each other.

Questions

1 Explain in what ways the USA and Britain disagreed with the USSR about: a) German reparations; b) monetary reform.

2 Read Source 4. What was the link between monetary reform and the Berlin airlift?

3 What do Sources 2 and 4 say were the reasons for the division of Germany?

4 Why did most West Berliners not want to become part of the Soviet zone? Why was the West ready to back them?

5 To what extent was the Soviet Union's fear of invasion responsible for the creation of East and West Germany?

3.2 The causes of the Cold War

There are three main explanations for the Cold War: the traditional, the revisionist and the post-revisionist.

The traditional explanation

Commentators such as the American, Kennan, argued in the late 1940s that Russian leaders had always distrusted foreigners and believed that the best form of defence against a dangerous world was to expand Soviet power (see Source 5 page 9). According to this theory, the Cold War was therefore mainly the fault of the USSR.

The revisionist explanation

Historians in the 1960s and 1970s argued that the USA underestimated the Soviet desire for security, and failed to realise how the US possession of the atomic bomb between 1945 and 1951 was regarded by the Soviet Union as a major threat. As the main revisionist historian, W. A. Williams, put it:

Source 7

W. A. Williams, *The Tragedy of American Diplomacy*, 1962.

Particularly after the atom bomb was created and used, American policy left the Soviets with but one option; either acquiesce in [agree to] American proposals or be confronted [faced] with American power and hostility.

So this view blames the Cold War mainly on the Americans.

The post-revisionist explanation

More recent historians avoid blaming either the USSR or the USA. They think that the situation in both Eastern and Western Europe was so complicated at the end of the war that it is not surprising that there were misunderstandings on both sides. As Martin McCauley puts it:

Source 8

Martin McCauley, *Origins of the Cold War*, 1983.

It [the post-revisionist interpretation] sees the situation as so . . . complex that no generalisation [general conclusion] about who was to blame will suffice [be enough].

Questions

1 Summarise the main differences between the three different interpretations of the causes of the Cold War.

2 Why do you think the first interpretation was the one most favoured in the West in the 1950s?

3 Why do you think many Western historians in the 1960s and 1970s became 'revisionists'?

4 Few Soviet primary sources have been available to Western historians. In what ways is this lack likely to have affected their interpretations?

5 On which interpretation of the Cold War do you think that the account on pages 6–11 in this book is based? Explain your answer.

Unit 4 · Tensions in Europe, 1949–1972

This Unit shows how the Cold War kept Europe in a state of tension throughout the 1950s and 1960s, preventing East and West from opening the 'Iron Curtain' between them.

NATO and the Warsaw Pact

To the strategy of the Truman Doctrine and the economics of the Marshall Plan, the West added in 1949 a military alliance, the North Atlantic Treaty Organisation (NATO). The major countries of Western Europe joined with the United States and Canada to provide armed forces to resist communist expansion in Europe.

The Soviet Union retaliated by getting its Eastern European allies to join Cominform (1947) which developed common anti-American policies, Comecon (1949) which supervised trade and economic matters, and the Warsaw Pact (1955) which was an anti-Western military alliance.

Source 1

Soviet cartoon of 1952 depicting NATO generals as goose-stepping latter-day Nazis.

Source 2

NATO poster.

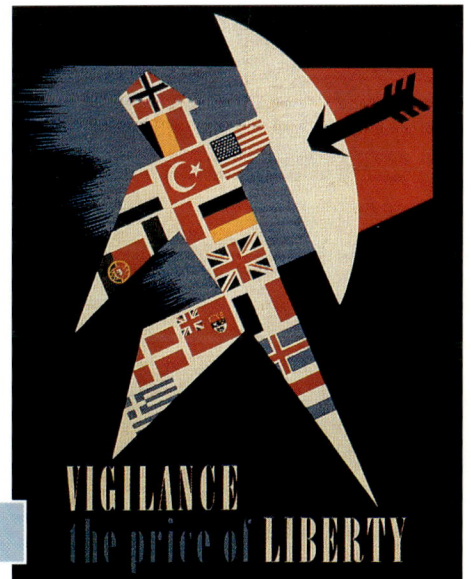

VIGILANCE the price of LIBERTY

Soviet control of Eastern Europe

The Soviet control of Eastern Europe lasted 40 years and never had popular support. There were risings in East Germany in 1953 and in Hungary and Poland in 1956. In 1961 the East German government had to build a wall across Berlin to prevent many of its citizens, including some of the most skilled, from fleeing to the West. In 1968 there was widespread unrest in Czechoslovakia.

Source 3

East German workers building
the Berlin Wall in 1961.

All these revolts were crushed by military action. The Moscow view was
that the whole of Eastern Europe had to stay loyal to the Soviet form of
communism. If one country succeeded in breaking away, the rest would
quickly follow. The best example of Soviet ruthlessness was in Hungary in
1956.

Source 4

A street in Budapest near the
end of the revolt in 1956.

Hungary, 1956

The Hungarians had no great love for the Soviet Union, nor for Rakosi's
communist government, which had executed 2,000 opponents and
imprisoned 200,000 more. When Stalin died in 1953 and was replaced in
the USSR by leaders such as Khrushchev, who criticised Stalin's methods,
Hungarian writers and students began openly to question the methods of
Rakosi's government and to call for the withdrawal of Soviet troops.
Economic problems fuelled anti-Soviet feelings and, on 23 October 1956,
the secret police (the AVH) fired on anti-government demonstrators,
killing hundreds.

A full-scale revolt erupted. Imre Nagy (pronounced 'Noj') became
Prime Minister. Khrushchev, hoping perhaps that the revolt would fizzle
out, ordered Soviet troops to retreat. Nagy, however, spurred on by the
enthusiasm of the demonstrating crowds, demanded not only that all
Soviet troops should leave, but also that Hungary should withdraw from
the Warsaw Pact. In addition, he said that he would order new free
elections. This was more than Khrushchev would tolerate. Poland and
East Germany were also restless. If Hungary gained so much
independence the whole of the Soviet control of Eastern Europe might
collapse. On 4 November 6,000 tanks and fifteen divisions of the Warsaw
Pact armies invaded Hungary, driving straight into Budapest. After ten
days' fighting the fierce Hungarian resistance was finally overcome:
20,000 Hungarians and 7,000 Soviet troops died.

Many Hungarians kept fighting in the hope that the West would come
to their aid. As the Soviets tightened their hold on Budapest, Hungarian
radio appealed to the world for help (Source 5).

Source 5

Budapest Radio, November 1956

Civilised peoples of the world! We implore you in the name of justice, freedom and . . . of active solidarity to help us. Our ship is sinking . . .. The shadows grow darker every hour over the soil of Hungary. Extend to us your fraternal aid.

No help came. The West was distracted and divided by the Anglo–French attack on Egypt. Soviet action against the leaders of the revolt was vile. Nagy and several of his associates were promised their freedom but kidnapped and secretly hanged two years later; 20,000 others were imprisoned and 200,000 fled into exile.

The Brezhnev Doctrine, 1968

The Czechoslovak rising of 1968 caused Brezhnev, Khrushchev's successor, to tell the world that the Soviet Union was ready to act in the interests of 'socialism' (communism) if it was threatened by Western capitalism. The Brezhnev Doctrine balanced the Truman Doctrine and the Cold War continued into the 1970s.

The arms race

The two superpowers raced against each other to produce the most up-to-date and destructive nuclear weapons. Both nations poured so much money and effort into nuclear technology that by 1970 they had enough weapons to destroy their enemy (and the whole world) many times over. This arms race did nothing to lessen the fears which had created the Cold War but prevented a real hot war because of the colossal destruction such a war would have caused.

Britain and France played their own smaller part in the arms race. They could not keep up with the superpowers but developed their own hydrogen bombs in the 1950s and continued to insist on having their own 'nuclear deterrent'. NATO and Warsaw Pact forces became armed with nuclear weapons and their commanders planned how a nuclear third world war might be fought.

The first signs that political leaders could see that the nuclear arms race was insane appeared in 1969, when Strategic Arms Limitation Talks (SALT) began between the USA and the USSR. The SALT 1 Agreement of 1972 restricted the development of anti-ballistic missiles. The success of SALT 1 led to more attempts to end the arms race.

Questions

1 What were: a) NATO; b) the Warsaw Pact; c) the Berlin Wall?

2 What do Sources 1 and 2 reveal about the attitudes of the East and West towards each other?

3 Why was there a revolt in Hungary in 1956?

4 Compare the Brezhnev Doctrine of 1968 with the Truman Doctrine of 1947.

Unit 5 · Towards Western unity, 1945–1972

5.1 First attempts at unity

The desire for a permanent peace

The movement towards greater European unity began among the many groups resisting the Nazis. Resistance leaders believed that the Nazi conquest and domination of Europe had been helped by the selfish nationalism of the European states. They dreamed of a post-war Europe united as a single organisation, working to preserve peace and to improve the wealth and living conditions of all its inhabitants. Many of them would have agreed with Jean Monnet, a member of the French National Liberation Committee which, while in exile in Algeria, organised the Resistance across France. He wrote in 1943:

Source 1

Jean Monnet, *Memoirs*, 1978.

There will be no peace in Europe if states re-establish themselves on the basis of national sovereignty [as independent nations] . . . they are too small to give to their people the prosperity which is now possible . . . they need wider markets . . ..To enjoy the prosperity and social progress that are essential, the states of Europe must form a federation . . . which will make them a single European unit.

Federation or confederation?

A federation is a country, such as the United States of America, which is made up of members who obey a single government on important matters, for example, defence and taxation, but keep some control over their own affairs in other matters, such as health or education. Monnet and his friends (see page 22) wanted to create a federal or United States of Europe with a strong government which was supranational, i.e. could tell national governments what to do. Others wanted a confederation, in which the links were looser and most powers remained with national governments. General de Gaulle, head of the French government in exile during the war, used the phrase *l'Europe des patries* (the Europe of fatherlands) to sum up his confederal attitude (see pages 25–26).

The Council of Europe

Immediately after the war Britain, in the person of Churchill, seemed to be giving the lead towards greater European unity. Between 1945 and 1949 conferences were held which led to defence agreements between Britain, France and Belgium, the Netherlands and Luxemburg and to the setting up of the Council of Europe in Strasburg in 1949.

Source 2

The Council of Europe building in Strasburg.

Strasburg was chosen as the home of the Council to symbolise the hopes for a new, peaceful Europe. It is the main city of Alsace-Lorraine, the cause of bitter conflicts between France and Germany in the past, and stands just inside France, looking across the Rhine to Germany.

The Council began with ten member states and a representative assembly. It discussed matters such as economics, education, culture and human rights. It could only advise and had no political power.

In fact Britain had no interest in becoming part of a federal Europe. Churchill at heart was hardly even a confederalist. He had a saying, 'We are with Europe, but not part of it'.

The OEEC

Economic need pushed the nations of Europe closer together. Immediately after the war the governments of Belgium, the Netherlands and Luxemburg (Benelux) had agreed to remove customs barriers between their three nations and to co-operate closely on economic matters. For Western Europe as a whole, a major step forward was the foundation of the Organisation of European Economic Co-operation (OEEC) in 1948 to decide how Marshall Aid should be spent (see page 10). Most of the nations of Western Europe were represented on its Council, to which the USA gave the responsibility of dividing up the Marshall Aid funds. This it did successfully and continued as an organisation in which important economic issues could be discussed.

Jean Monnet

The person who did most to set Western Europe on the path to greater unity was Jean Monnet. He was born in 1888, the son of a French brandy-seller. A brilliant organiser, he made his name during the First World War by helping to keep the joint supply systems of the French and British armies running. In 1919 he became Deputy Secretary-General of the new

League of Nations but soon left to pursue a successful international business career, particularly in the USA. During the Second World War he worked closely with de Gaulle in exile. After the defeat of Germany the French government first asked him to prepare a plan to repair and modernise the French economy and then, in 1947, appointed him to put the plan into action.

Monnet, a keen federalist, believed that the best route towards greater political union and recovery of Europe was through economic co-operation.

Source 3

Jean Monnet, *The United States of Europe has Begun* (a collection of speeches made between 1952 and 1954), 1955.

The creation of a large internal market is essential to make it possible for Europeans to take their place in the world again.

Questions

1 Why did so many of the wartime leaders of Western Europe support the idea of greater European unity?

2 What is the difference between a federation and a confederation?

3 How did Churchill's ideas for Europe differ from those of Monnet?

5.2   From the ECSC to the Treaty of Rome

The ECSC

Monnet knew many powerful people in both Europe and America and was good at persuading them to his way of thinking. He also had an excellent sense of timing. He was encouraged by the success of the OEEC and of the Benelux economic co-operation. In 1950 he drew up a plan to link together in one organisation the coal and steel industries of Western Europe. This he sent to Robert Schuman, the French Foreign Minister. Schuman backed the plan since he, too, was a keen federalist and wanted to bind together the old enemies, France and West Germany, as closely and as quickly as possible. At a press conference in May 1950, Schuman declared that the French and West German governments would be:

Source 4

Peter Lane, *Europe Since 1945*, 1985.

Placing the whole of Franco-German coal and steel output under a common High Authority, in an organisation open . . . to other countries of Europe. The pooling of coal and steel production . . . will be a first step in the federation of Europe . . . . [This action] will make it plain that any war between France and Germany becomes not only unthinkable . . . but impossible.

Source 5

Jean Monnet (left) and Robert Schuman at the first meeting of the ECSC in Luxemburg. 8 September 1950.

On the border between France and Luxemburg, 10 February 1953. This train, carrying the flags of the six member states, celebrates the start of the ECSC.

France, West Germany, Italy and Benelux all joined the European Coal and Steel Community (ECSC). They agreed to a High Authority which was supranational (i.e. above national organisations), made up of representatives from all six member states which developed the coal and steel industries for them all. Britain was invited to join, but turned down the invitation (see page 27).

The ECSC was the first clear step towards a federal Europe. Obviously it owed much to Monnet, who became the first President of the ECSC's High Authority, and to Schuman; but also to Paul-Henri Spaak, Foreign Minister of Belgium and Alcide de Gasperi, Prime Minister of Italy. All wanted a federal Europe.

The ECSC was an economic success. Though it did not find modernising the coal industry an easy task, steel production increased by 42 per cent in five years, faster than its main competitors. The supranational High Authority also worked well enough to give confidence to the European federalists.

Although another federal project, the European Defence Community (EDC), failed in 1953, the federalists pushed ahead. In 1955 the foreign ministers of the ECSC 'Six' met at Messina in Italy to discuss a Benelux plan to extend the idea of the ECSC across the whole economic life of the Six. They aimed to create a common market without customs barriers between the member-states. A supranational authority would develop the economic policies of the area, which in population and wealth would rival the USA. From economic co-operation, political union would follow.

The Treaty of Rome, 1957

Monnet formed an Action Committee to persuade public opinion of the value of such a common market but the person who did most to make it a reality was Paul-Henri Spaak. He led the committee which turned the ideas outlined in the Messina Conference into proposals that could be approved by the six member governments. He was helped by two major crises in 1956, the first the failure of the Anglo-French attack on Egypt over the Suez Canal and the second the Soviet invasion of Hungary (see page 18). Both these events made Western Europeans feel that they were living in a continuously dangerous world and that their safety lay in greater unity. In March 1957 representatives of the Six met in Rome to sign a treaty agreeing to create a European Economic Community or common market between them during the next twelve to fifteen years.

Questions

1. What were the OEEC, the ECSC, the EDC and the EEC?

2. What changes did the ECSC bring to the coal and steel industries of Western Europe? Why was it so important for European unity?

3. What hopes had the governments of the Six when they signed the Treaty of Rome in 1957?

5.3   The EEC, 1957–1973

The European Economic Community had four important parts:
- A supranational Commission to deal with the day to day work of the EEC.
- A Council representing the six governments which made sure that the Commission did not move too far or fast for the national governments.
- A Parliamentary Assembly whose democratically elected members were able to comment on and criticise the work of the Commission.
- A Court of Justice whose seven judges would decide when arguments took place about the way the Treaty was supposed to work.

The Six also created a body known as Euratom to develop jointly a European nuclear industry.

The Treaty of Rome was a remarkable achievement by the federalists. As Spaak explained in 1964:

Source 7

Paul-Henri Spaak, speech to the Council of Europe Assembly, 1964.

Those who drew up the Treaty of Rome . . . did not think of it as essentially economic; they thought of it as a stage on the way to political union; . . . [If] it is bound to happen so much the better; but it is wiser to work steadily and urgently to make it happen.

Two rivals: the EEC and EFTA

Economically the EEC was an immediate success and progressed well throughout the 1960s. Tariffs (customs duties paid on goods at national frontiers) became fewer and lower. Rules preventing money from moving from one member country to another were relaxed and people could more easily take up jobs anywhere in the EEC. The Six agreed a common agricultural policy (CAP) which, though it became very expensive and controversial in the 1970s, encouraged high levels of production from European farmers and protected them from overseas competition. The Six also began to consider how best to achieve a common monetary system.

Source 8

The EEC and EFTA as seen by the British cartoonist, Low.

Source 9

A big Common Market firm that did well in the 1960s was the FIAT motor company of Italy. This is the FIAT factory in Turin. Note the car testing track on the roof.

Although invited by the Six to join with them in creating the Common Market, Britain again stayed aloof (see pages 27–29). However, the rapid appearance and economic success of the EEC caused the British government to approach other countries to create a rival trading organisation, the European Free Trade Association (EFTA) in 1959. EFTA had seven members – Britain, Denmark, Norway, Sweden, Austria, Switzerland and Portugal. Its aim was simply to reduce customs duties between member states, not to develop common economic policies. Britain's hope in setting up EFTA was to persuade the Six of the EEC to co-operate with Britain in looser, less federal schemes. It did not have this effect. Rather it split Western Europe into two rival parts.

Source 10

Europe in 1959.

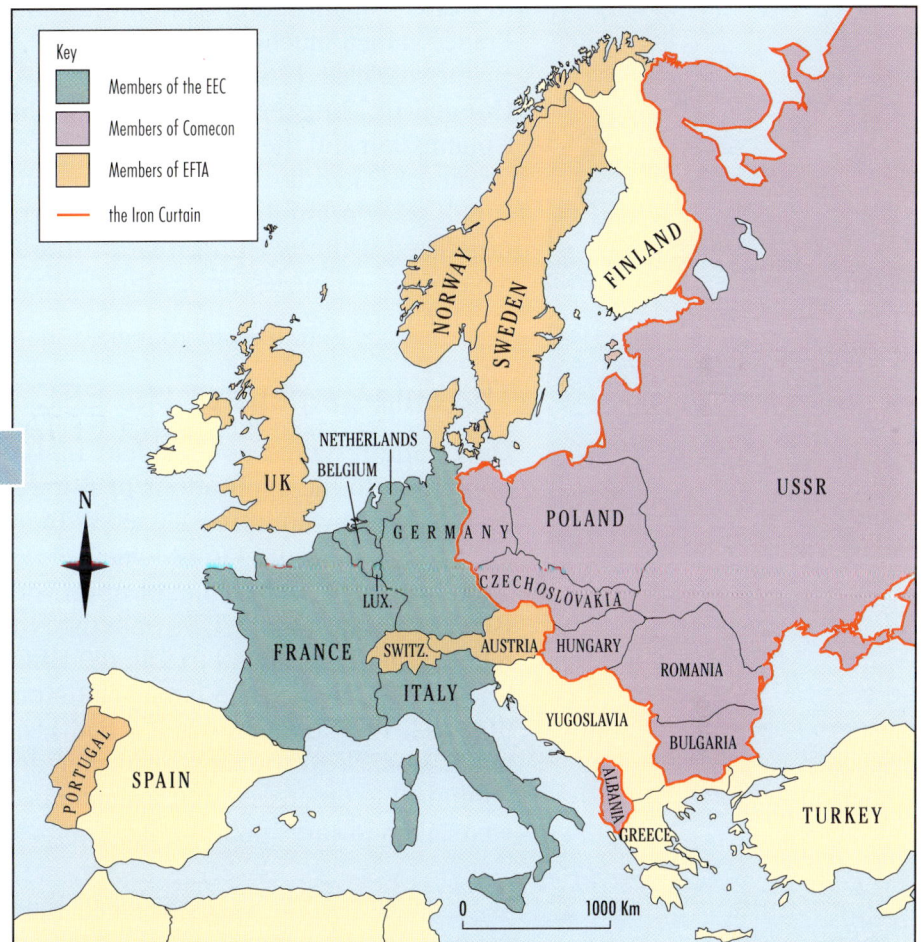

Key

Members of the EEC

Members of Comecon

Members of EFTA

the Iron Curtain

De Gaulle, Britain and the EEC

Politically the 1960s were a very bumpy period for the EEC, mainly because of General de Gaulle, President of France from 1958 to 1969. He came to power as a result of an immense political crisis which had erupted because of the failure of the politicians of the Fourth Republic to solve the problem of Algeria, France's most important colony. De Gaulle, who had led the Free French armies during the liberation of France, was seen as the one man who could save the country from chaos. He insisted on a new constitution, that of the Fifth Republic, which gave the President many powers which he used to the full.

Source 11

President de Gaulle on tour in France in 1968. A typical pose.

De Gaulle had a deep belief in the greatness of France and always put France's interests first. He vetoed (refused to agree to) Britain's first application to join the EEC in 1963, although the other five members were strongly in favour. He also vetoed the second application in 1967 (see page 29). He again opposed his other five partners, this time in 1965, when they wished to increase the powers of the European Commission and Parliament at the expense of the Council of Ministers. De Gaulle would have nothing to do with such federal measures. He said that they would lead to a situation in which member countries would lose their national identities and irresponsible bureaucrats would take over. When the other five pressed ahead, de Gaulle withdrew the French representatives from the Council of Ministers for seven months, throwing the EEC's organisation into confusion. However, de Gaulle knew that France gained much from the EEC and had no intention of destroying it. By the so-called 'Luxemburg compromise' of 1966, France returned to the Council of Ministers while the five slimmed-down their plans for the Commission and the Parliament.

The EEC had been tested but not badly damaged. It remained able to speak with a single voice on important matters. Internationally it negotiated with the USA on tariffs (the Kennedy Round, 1967), and with developing countries on trading links (the Yaounde Convention, 1963 and the Lome Agreements of 1975).

The enlargement of the EEC

De Gaulle resigned as President in 1969. With his departure, French opposition to the applications of Britain, Denmark, Ireland and Norway ended. All four countries signed a Treaty of Accession in January 1972 and the Six seemed set to become Ten. However, while the parliaments of Britain, Ireland and Denmark approved the Treaty, Norway stayed out. Bitter opposition to the EEC split the Norwegian political parties and in a referendum the proposal to join the EEC was defeated by a small margin. So the Six only became Nine. The Norwegian referendum was the first time that the Common Market had been rejected by anyone and was a major setback to the idea of further union. During the 1970s the EEC continued to progress towards greater economic unity but no further steps were taken towards political unity.

Questions

1   What were the differences between the EEC and EFTA? Why did the former become so successful while the latter had little effect?

2   Did de Gaulle help or hinder European unity?

3   a) Describe the progress Western Europe made towards (i) economic union and (ii) political union between 1949 and 1967.
b) In your opinion, was it more successful politically or economically? Explain your thinking.

4   a) In what ways did the EEC change between 1957 and 1973?
b) How far was it from being the United States of Europe in 1973?

Unit 6 · Britain and Europe, 1945–1975

6.1   Britain and Europe in the 1940s and 1950s

One of the most important and difficult questions for British governments in the second half of the 20th century was what kind of links they should have with Europe. It was a question which caused deep divisions within the Conservative and Labour parties, and the general public too.

1945–1956: Britain as a world power

Anne Deighton, a historian, sums up well the thinking in Britain in 1945:

Source 1

Anne Deighton, 'Missing the boat: Britain and Europe 1945–61', an article in *The Contemporary Record,* February 1990.

> . . . there was a consensus of views [general agreement] that Britain was still a great power. Her experience of war was quite different from that of her continental neighbours – she had been unoccupied, undefeated. British diplomats had sat at the high table of wartime conferences, and Britain now occupied the German zone that included the wealthy Ruhr region – a key to European recovery.

Churchill (and Attlee's Labour government agreed with him) believed that Britain had world-wide responsibilities, divided into three main overlapping areas; the USA, the Empire/Commonwealth, and Europe.

Churchill (see page 6) encouraged the movement towards European unity between 1945 and 1955 but believed that Britain, with its proud empire and enjoying a special relationship with the USA, should always remain separate.

Britain and the ECSC, 1950

So it was not surprising that Britain refused to join the ECSC. A British government would never put its vital economic interests under the control of a supranational organisation. As Morrison, Deputy Prime Minister of the Labour government, put it:

Source 2

Alistair Horne, *Macmillan, 1894–1956,* 1988.

> It is no good. We can't do it. The Durham miners won't wear it.

The Messina Conference and the Treaty of Rome

The same attitudes still existed in 1955, though by then the Conservatives were in power. Advised by the Foreign Office, the government treated the Messina Conference as a minor affair, sending an official as an observer not as a representative. Foreign Office officials believed that the EEC was unlikely to come into existence and if it did, it would not work. They were wrong on both counts.

Source 3

Cartoon from the German magazine *Simplicissimus*, 1961. Macmillan is the passenger in the boat which is being rowed by Erhard, the West German Economics Minister. De Gaulle is the sailor on the ship *Europa*.

■ Explain the cartoon. What is the attitude of the artist towards Britain?

1957–1963: A rethink

In 1961, Harold Macmillan, Prime Minister of a Conservative government, applied to the EEC for entry. There were four main reasons for this major change in British policy. The first was the success of the EEC, greater and faster than the government's advisers had predicted. The second was the weakening of Commonwealth links. Trends in world trade showed that the Commonwealth was becoming economically less important and Europe more important to Britain. Thirdly, the Suez Crisis of 1956 proved that Britain was no longer a world power and could not rely on its special relationship with the USA. Britain and France had tried to end by force an Egyptian take-over of the Suez Canal and had failed because of the opposition of the rest of the world, led by the USA. The Americans anyway wanted a more united Europe. Fourthly, the EEC was forging closer and closer links between its members. The longer Britain stayed outside, the harder entry would become. As Macmillan put it in his speech to the House of Commons in August 1961:

Source 4

Hansard Parliamentary Debates, 2 August 1961.

. . . most of us recognise that in a changing world if we are not to be left behind and to drop out of the mainstream of the world's life, we must be prepared to change and adapt our methods. All through history this has been one of the main sources of our strength.

Questions

1. What part in world affairs did most British politicians believe that Britain should play in 1945?

2. Why did they take this view?

3. How and for what reasons had many politicians changed their minds by 1962?

6.2 The EEC in the 1960s

The first French veto, 1963

Macmillan expected the British application to succeed, but he misjudged de Gaulle. The General planned to dominate the Six through a close alliance with West Germany. To include Britain would weaken France's position. Moreover, he was strongly anti-American and believed that the British would still act for the USA once they were members of the EEC. A recent deal on nuclear weapons (the Nassau Agreement) between Macmillan and President Kennedy had angered him greatly.

At a special press conference in January 1963, in front of 500 journalists and 300 guests, de Gaulle vetoed Britain's entry. He said:

Source 5

J. Lacouture, *De Gaulle the Ruler 1945–70*, 1993.

Britain is an island, bound by its trade . . . with the most varied and distant countries . . . the nature, structure, circumstances, peculiar to England are different from those of other continentals. How can Britain, in the way that she lives, produces, trades, be included in the Common Market as it has been planned and as it functions? . . . [An enlarged EEC] would not last for very long and . . . would seem like a colossal Atlantic community under American direction, and that is not at all what France wants . . ..

Source 6

President de Gaulle during the 'No' press conference, 15 January 1963.

It was a bad setback for Macmillan. He noted in his diary:

Source 7

Alistair Horne, *Macmillan, 1856–86*, 1988.

All our policies at home and abroad are in ruins . . .. The great question remains 'What is the alternative?' to the European Community. If we are honest, we must say that there is none . . ..

The second French veto, 1967

Harold Wilson, who led the Labour Party to victory in the general election of 1964, had opposed the 1962 application but as Prime Minister he came round to Macmillan's way of thinking. The Commonwealth continued to weaken as more of the old colonies won their independence. The special relationship with the USA did not appear to amount to much. While the EEC continued to prosper, the British economy struggled from crisis to crisis. Wilson formally applied for membership in August 1967. De Gaulle was unmoved. His second veto followed in November. In his opinion, Britain was still not yet ready.

6.3 Getting in and staying in, 1967–1975

Source 8

Pro- and anti-EEC demonstrators meet in Trafalgar Square, 1971.

Britain joins the EEC

De Gaulle resigned in 1969 and his departure removed the main obstacle to Britain's entry within Europe. Heath's Conservative government which won the 1970 general election applied again to join the EEC. A Treaty of Accession was agreed in 1972 which had to be approved by the British parliament. It had a stormy passage. Both the Conservative and Labour parties were split and, on one critical vote, the pro-EEC majority was down to just four votes. However, the Treaty was eventually ratified and Britain, with Denmark and Ireland, finally became a member of the EEC on 1 January 1973.

The 1975 referendum

However, the drama was not yet over. Although Wilson, the Labour leader, had applied for Britain's membership in 1967, the majority of the Labour Party voted against the Treaty of Accession in 1972. Then Labour won the 1974 election. Though Wilson and most of his Cabinet ministers favoured staying in the EEC, so great was the opposition of sections of the Labour Party that Wilson agreed to a referendum. The Labour Party was split in half on the issue but the Conservatives and Liberals were strongly in favour. So were most British industrialists and farmers. In the referendum the voting was 67 per cent in favour of staying in the EEC and 33 per cent against. Wilson's aim in holding the referendum was to keep Labour in power and Britain in the EEC. It was a clever tactic, which worked out exactly as he had planned.

The large pro-EEC majority ended the debate for the next ten years. However, deep suspicions about the Common Market remained with some British politicians, including Margaret Thatcher, the Conservative Prime Minister from 1979 to 1990.

Problems with Britain's role in the EEC resurfaced between 1987 and 1993 under the leadership of Thatcher and her successor, John Major (see Unit 8).

Source 9

Vicky's cartoon shows Dean Acheson (far right) with the US President Kennedy looking at a little British lion overshadowed by a German eagle and a French cock.

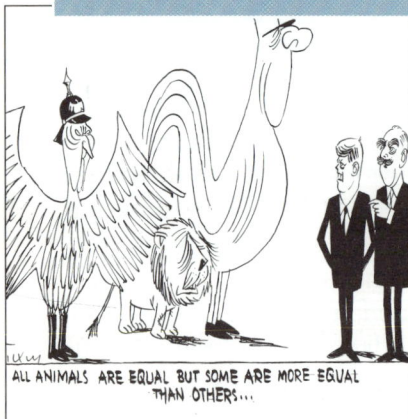

ALL ANIMALS ARE EQUAL BUT SOME ARE MORE EQUAL THAN OTHERS…

The Common Market debate

The question whether or not Britain should join the EEC had aroused tremendous passions. It forced Britons to think about vital issues such as national independence, their history, the quality of their way of life and the best way forward into the future. At the end of the 1950s, the nation was at a crossroads, bewildered and sensitive. When in a speech in 1962, Dean Acheson, an experienced American politician and friend of Britain, remarked that Britain had lost an Empire and not yet found a role, the fury with which the British press greeted this remark, the truth of which was clear to most of the rest of the world, showed that he had touched a raw nerve.

For some, joining the EEC was the best way forward for Britain. Iain Macleod, a minister in Macmillan's Conservative government, said:

Source 10

Ian Macleod's speech in his Enfield constituency, 1962.

We believe that Britain ought to play her full part in the great movement towards European unity . . .. It will not prove an easy road to prosperity. It will be hard but rewarding. Out of date practices will have to go. But as a nation we should thrill to the challenge . . .. Our people are inventive and skilful; our agriculture is efficient and competitive. Our industry will respond to the challenge of competition and to high rewards for success.

Others believed that entry would be a bad mistake:

Source 11

Labour leader Hugh Gaitskell at the Labour Party Conference, 1962.

[Entry] . . . would mean selling the Commonwealth down the river . . . [By handing over powers to supranational authorities such as the European Commission] it would mean the end of a thousand years of history . . ..

Another Labour worry was that the EEC would allow too much power to businesses buying and selling in a free market. Powerful companies might make it harder for governments to carry out economic policies which would benefit all citizens, especially the working people.

Source 12

Aneurin Bevan in the Labour journal *Tribune*, 1957.

Are we expected to go back almost a century, reject Socialism and clasp free trade to our bosom as though it were the one solution of our social evils? . . . Socialists cannot at one and the same time call for economic planning and accept the verdict of free competition, no matter how extensive the area it covers. The jungle is not made more acceptable just because it is almost limitless.

To friendly foreigners, the question was much easier to answer. Here is Jean Monnet, commenting on the result of the 1975 referendum:

Source 13

Jean Monnet, *Memoirs*, 1978.

[It] . . . set the seal on what was already obvious. Great Britain had no choice . . . except solitary decline or integration into a larger grouping . . ..That had been obvious for 25 years; but it takes a good quarter of a century to end the illusions which dead realities leave in the minds of nations and of men.

Questions

1. What are the main arguments put forward by Macmillan (Sources 4 and 7) and by Macleod in Source 10 for joining the EEC?

2. Gaitskell (Source 11) and Bevan (Source 12) use quite different arguments for staying out of the EEC. What are these?

3. Why were Gaitskell and other opponents of the EEC worried about the supranational character of the EEC (Source 11)? How important do you think full national independence is in the modern world?

4. Was Monnet (Source 13) correct in his view that Britain had no choice but to join the EEC or face 'solitary decline'? Explain your thinking.

7.1 Eastern Europe transformed, 1948–1970

Economic dependence

Once the communist take-over was complete by 1948 (see pages 7–8) Eastern Europe was economically transformed. Most major industries and services were nationalised. Private ownership was abolished and replaced by state control. Governments produced five-year plans which set national and local targets for economic growth, with the rapid build-up of industry as the priority. As Source 1 shows, they had, for the most part, real success in achieving higher industrial production.

Source 1

Taken from L. P. Morris, *Eastern Europe in 1945*, 1983. Note that such statistics, though they reflect trends and make possible rough comparisons, should be used with caution.

Iron production in millions of tons			
	1949	**1960**	**1970**
Bulgaria	1.5	N/A	1.2
Czechoslovakia	1.6	4.7	7.5
East Germany	.2	2.0	2.0
Poland	1.2	4.6	7.3
Electricity in MWh			
Bulgaria	.6	4.7	19.5
Czechoslovakia	7.5	24.5	45.2
East Germany	14.5	40.3	67.8
Poland	7.5	29.3	64.5

Source 2

Polish women working on the railways, 1956.

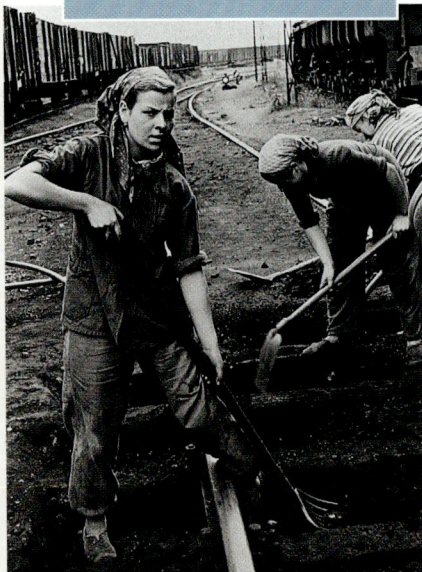

Social developments

Economic transformation was matched by major social developments. Communist governments valued education highly. Illiteracy rates fell sharply. Vocational education flourished and there was an enormous expansion of university education, with science and technology the priority.

Medical services expanded impressively. They were free and initially aimed at mothers, children and the urban working population. Diseases such as tuberculosis and malaria were wiped out and the life expectancy of the population moved towards Western standards.

Most employees in the medical and education services were female and an ever-increasing number of women went out to work. Maternity leave regulations, creches and kindergartens helped women continue in work. However, the standing of women in Eastern European society did not obviously improve. They did not get equal pay for equal work, nor did they gain an increasing share of top jobs.

Source 3

Heavy industry (and heavy pollution) in Romania, 1990.

House-building did not keep pace with the movement of people from the countryside into the towns and by the 1960s there was a severe housing crisis all over Eastern Europe. State building schemes were clearly failing. In the 1960s and 1970s most governments gave housing a much higher priority and were prepared to encourage private builders.

Eastern European governments valued industrial production and public services higher than the standard of living of ordinary people and could usually ignore public opinion. Living standards generally fell in the early 1950s, improved later in that decade, stagnated during the 1960s and improved again in the 1970s. They remained much lower than in Western Europe.

Source 4

Table taken from W. Laqueur, *Europe Since Hitler*, 1982.

Number of inhabitants per private motor car.

	1950	1960	1970
East Germany	242	54	15
Hungary	715	319	43
Poland	771	253	68
Britain	21	9	5

Questions

1 What do the figures in Source 1 tell you about the industrial performance of: a) Bulgaria; b) Poland?

2 Why do you think historians such as Morris (Source1) think iron and electricity figures are a useful measure of industrial production?

3 What does Source 3 tell you about the economic thinking of the Romanian government?

4 To what extent did communist governments of Eastern Europe improve: a) industrial production; b) public services; c) living standards; d) the position of women, between 1950 and 1970? Would you expect their policies to have made them more or less popular in 1970 than in 1950? Explain your thinking.

7.2   Changes in Western Europe, 1945–1973

Rapid and prolonged economic growth

For the nations of Western Europe the 25 years from 1948 to 1973 were the time of the fastest and longest economic growth ever in their history – 'the golden economic summer' is how one recent historian has described it. Source 5 shows the extent of this growth.

Source 5

Table taken from W. Laqueur, *Europe Since Hitler*, 1982.

Index of industrial production 1938–1967. This table gives comparisons with industrial production in 1958 (100). For example, in 1938 West Germany produced 53 per cent of its 1958 production and, in 1967, 158 per cent.

	1938	1948	1952	1958	1959	1963	1967
West Germany	53	27	61	100	107	137	158
France	52	55	70	100	101	129	155
Italy	43	44	64	100	112	166	212
Sweden	52	74	81	100	106	140	176
Britain	67	74	84	100	105	119	133
USA	33	73	90	100	113	133	168
Japan	58	22	50	100	120	212	347

There were many reasons for this growth. The first was the need to repair the war damage and the readiness of the USA to provide Marshall Aid at a critical moment. This got the Western European economy moving. It kept going thanks to a number of factors. First of all, a rising population needed more schools, hospitals, roads and houses. Secondly, world trade expanded, helped by lower customs duties. Thirdly, there was a steady financial system held in place by the Bretton Woods Agreement of 1944 between the USA and other leading industrial nations. Lastly, and perhaps most important, cheap energy from the vast oil reserves of the Middle East was controlled by American and European oil companies.

Another important feature was the readiness of governments to plan for and encourage economic growth. Influenced by the writings of the British economist, J. M. Keynes, they believed that by using taxes and government spending on such things as hospitals and roads, they could keep their economies growing and avoid the high levels of unemployment of the 1930s.

Source 6

The Welfare State in action. A Swedish hospital in the late 1960s.

The Welfare State

Much of the new wealth created in these years went on services which the state provided to improve the welfare of its citizens, notably on medical services, education and pensions. All the nations of Western Europe had their version of the Welfare State. Those of Britain and Sweden were perhaps the most wide-ranging, while West Germany was especially generous on pensions and France on sickness benefit.

The new wealth and the growing welfare services brought far-reaching changes to Western European society. One population shift took place from the countryside to the cities and another from the inner cities to the suburbs. Workers' wages rose, so did educational standards. The Welfare State created a new range of jobs and the old class system began to crumble. In this increasingly affluent society, individuals of all ages and social backgounds spent a lower proportion of their income on necessities such as food and housing and had more to spend on 'luxuries' – washing machines, televisions, records, clothes and, above all, motor cars.

Source 7

A British advertisement for an Italian car from the 1960s.

Women

Between 1950 and 1970 the number of Western European women in paid employment increased substantially. But as in Eastern Europe they seldom enjoyed equal pay for equal work and rarely broke through to the top jobs. In politics their position if anything worsened. In France there were 30 female French deputies in the National Assembly in 1945, dropping to 10 in 1977, while in Britain women made up less than 3 per cent of MPs between 1945 and 1970. Spreading from the USA and gathering strength from the student unrest of the late 1960s, the feminist movement for equal rights for women gained momentum.

Youth culture and power

Two other features of the affluent society of the 1960s were the fast growth of the student population of Western Europe and the appearance of a self-conscious youth culture, whose highly critical views of the older generation gained much attention from the media. In the United States students became heavily involved in the protests against the Vietnam War.

They also angrily demonstrated against the big business corporations which supported the war. Many young Americans rebelled against their parents, regarding them as too alike, too concerned with their neighbours' views and lacking in adventure. Experimenting with drugs and living sexually free in communes were ways of protesting against that conformity.

Student unrest, 1968

In Europe overcrowded universities fuelled unrest. There too, students demonstrated against the Vietnam War and protested against the ways in which, in their opinion, modern society was making people conform and disliked those who wanted to go their own way. The authorities – university officials, police and governments – were the enemy.

The unrest was most serious in France. Some universities had expanded too fast and student conditions were poor. De Gaulle's popularity was falling. The country, wrote one journalist, was 'bored'. Plans for university reform, unpopular with some students, led to the occupation of first Nanterre in the suburbs of Paris and then the Sorbonne in the centre of the city. Early in May 1968 a bungled attempt by the police to end the Sorbonne occupation by force brought thousands of demonstrators onto the streets of Paris. Barricades went up and a fortnight of street-fighting followed, the heavily armed police being met by students hurling cobblestones.

Anti-government strikes swept the country. For a moment de Gaulle seemed to lose his nerve and thought of resigning, but, after a secret meeting with his army chiefs, he decided to remain. He called a general election, asking the nation to choose between himself and order or communism and anarchy. This action was enough to end the student revolt. Now the Gaullists demonstrated in the streets in favour of law and order and de Gaulle won a huge majority in the general election.

The 1973 oil crisis and the 1974–1976 recession

The golden economic summer ended in 1973 when the oil-producing countries of the Middle East quadrupled the price of oil, following the Yom Kippur War between Israel and the Arab states. In the 1960s the average annual growth rate of Western industrial nations had been 4.8 per cent. Between 1974 and 1976 it fell virtually to nothing. Though some recovery took place in the later 1970s both high unemployment and inflation reappeared as serious problems.

Source 8

Students confront the police in the streets of Paris, May 1968.

Questions

1 What were the main reasons for the economic growth of Western Europe between 1945 and 1973?

2 Compare the main economic and social changes which happened in Western Europe with those of Eastern Europe.

3 How did European women fare economically and socially in the 1950s and 1960s?

4 What were the student protests which came to a head in 1968 really about? How far did they change the politics of Western Europe?

Unit 8 · New challenges, 1973–1993

8.1 The Iron Curtain opens

The end of an era: boy with part of the broken Berlin Wall.

The Berlin Wall, the most hated symbol of the Cold War, was built in August 1961. Not for another 30 years would East Berliners be able to walk freely into West Berlin. The Wall was opened in November 1991. Its opening, followed by its rapid destruction by the citizens of Berlin, showed the world that the Cold War was at last over.

Changes within the Soviet Union

During the 1970s Soviet leaders sometimes seemed ready to be more friendly with the West in order to lessen the danger and the cost of the nuclear arms race. In 1972 the USSR and USA signed the first Strategic Arms Limitation Treaty (SALT 1) which was followed by SALT II in 1979. Also, at the Helsinki Conference of 1975, Brezhnev seemed ready to talk both about reducing the danger of war and about giving Russian people who disagreed with communism greater freedom to express their views.

However, the thaw ended in 1979 when Soviet forces invaded Afghanistan to keep in power the unpopular communist government there. Within the Soviet Union those who criticised the government, the 'dissidents', were harshly treated. In protest against the Soviet invasion of Afghanistan, the USA and some of its allies refused to send athletes to the 1980 Olympics which were held in Moscow.

Things began to change considerably within the Soviet Union when Mikhail Gorbachev became the Soviet leader in 1985. Gorbachev was sure that most Soviet citizens so disliked the way in which they were ruled that the only method of solving the immense economic and social problems which the country faced was to have greater freedom, democracy and reform. Key words for him were *glasnost* (open-ness) and *perestroika* (economic reconstruction). He also realised that the Soviet Union could not afford the costs of the Cold War.

The end of the Cold War

In 1987 Gorbachev visited Washington and signed a major arms reduction treaty with President Reagan. Two years later he pulled Soviet troops out of Afghanistan and with the new American President George Bush agreed further disarmament measures. They met on the island of Malta and together declared that as far as the two superpowers were concerned the Cold War had ended.

Like many reformers, Gorbachev set in motion forces too strong for him to control. Because he so weakened the power of the Communist Party within the Soviet Union, the Union fell apart. Its various republics such as the Ukraine, Russia and Georgia wanted much greater freedom and were only prepared to belong to a much looser confederation, the Commonwealth of Independent States. For their part, the Baltic republics of Estonia, Latvia and Lithuania insisted on complete independence. In December 1991 Gorbachev resigned as President of the Soviet Union, which had effectively ceased to exist.

Eastern Europe, 1970–1993

The 1970s saw much unrest in Eastern Europe. Poland had many demonstrations and strikes, the shipyard workers of Gdansk often taking the lead. The Czechs, too, refused to stay silent, despite their experiences of 1968. In 1977 a group campaigning for greater freedom published in Prague its Charter '77. In 1980 Solidarity, the Polish freedom movement led by Lech Walesa, organised further strikes and demonstrations. It built up its membership to more than 10 million and, though its leaders were harassed by the communist government, refused to end its demands for reform.

The effects of the Gorbachev reforms, 1985–1993

As soon as it became clear that Gorbachev was a serious reformer and that the Communist Party within the Soviet Union was growing weaker, the confidence of the anti-communist movements in Eastern Europe soared. Meanwhile, the communist governments, which were hugely unpopular, became increasingly anxious. Suddenly in 1989 infectious popular uprisings destroyed the communist control of Eastern Europe. Poland and Hungary led the way. In February Solidarity forced the communist leaders to sit down with it to discuss the future of Poland. In a June general election it won a landslide victory. By 1990 Walesa was Poland's President. Hungary had for some years been pursuing reforming economic policies and its communist rulers, like Gorbachev, hoped that by increasing the freedom of its citizens, they would hold on to their support. However, like Gorbachev, they were swept out of power as soon as genuine free elections were held in 1990.

Meanwhile, in September 1989, the Hungarian government had opened up its borders with Austria and Austria had opened its borders with East Germany. East Germans now could escape to the West via Czechoslovakia and Hungary. Thousands did so.

Mass demonstrations in cities such as Leipzig and Dresden caused the opening up both of the Berlin Wall and of the Iron Curtain across Germany. The communist governments of East Germany, Czechoslovakia and Bulgaria all resigned in November 1989. By October 1990 Germany had been reunified.

Only in Romania did the hated dictator Ceausescu try to hold on to power by force. He was overthrown in a violent revolution in December 1989 in which hundreds were killed. He and his wife were executed by a firing squad.

Problems following the 1989 revolutions

The end of communist rule in Central and Eastern Europe allowed several long-standing but hidden problems to reappear. The most

Source 2

Central and Eastern Europe in 1993.

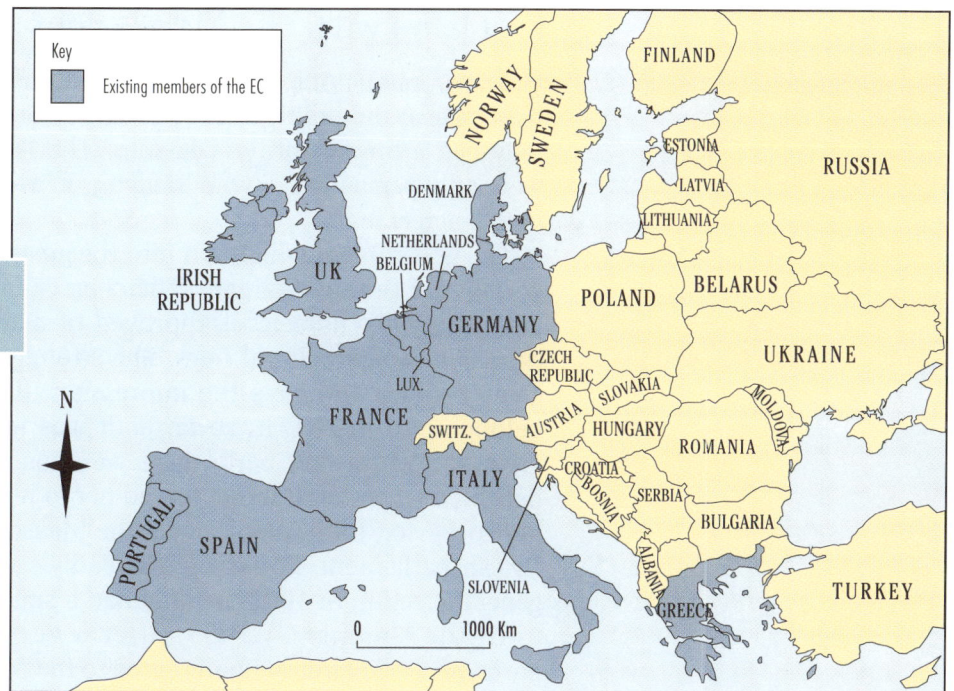

Key
- Existing members of the EC

dangerous were national rivalries. The former republics of the Soviet Union were soon threatening each other. The Slovaks parted company with the Czechs at the end of 1992. Yugoslavia fell apart as first Slovenia, then Croatia declared independence and Serbs, Croats and Muslims began an especially cruel war over Bosnia-Herzegovina in 1992 (see Source 2).

Economically, the change from communism to more capitalist methods proved painful. In Russia there were desperate food shortages and throughout Eastern Europe unemployment and inflation reached dangerous levels.

8.2   Western European unity, 1975–1993

The European Community (as the EEC was renamed in 1967) continued to attract new members. Greece joined in 1981, Portugal and Spain in 1985. It continued to prosper, averaging a 3.4 per cent annual growth rate in the 1970s. However it did not do as well as in the 1960s. Growth slowed, unemployment and inflation increased. Three times, in 1973, 1979 and 1991, there were periods of serious economic recession.

Nonetheless, among the EC officials and some European politicians enthusiasm for greater unity remained. In 1979 the European Monetary System was introduced and ideas for a common currency began actively to be discussed. In 1986 the Single European Act was agreed. This by 1992 further reduced the barriers between the different member states to make possible the free movement of goods, persons, services and capital. Between 1988 and 1991, Jacques Delors, President of the European Commission, encouraged by most EC governments, made suggestions for closer union. In December 1991 at an EC 'summit' meeting at Maastricht in the Netherlands, all the leaders of the member states of the EC agreed to move towards greater monetary and political co-operation.

Problems with the Maastricht Treaty

However, public opinion about the Maastricht Treaty was less favourable than that of the political leaders. The French (normally keen on the EC) only had a tiny majority in favour. The Danes first voted against it and were only persuaded to vote in favour in a second referendum by changes in the agreement.

The government which ran into the greatest difficulties over Maastricht was that of Britain. Margaret Thatcher, Conservative Prime Minister from 1979 to 1990, fiercely disapproved of many of the policies of the EC, especially its agricultural ones. She strongly opposed any moves towards greater union and gave the impression that she was only interested in belonging to the EC in so far as it was in Britain's interests to do so. However, within her party there were many keen Europeans who were delighted when her Cabinet forced her to resign in 1990. It was the task of her successor, John Major, to get the Maastricht agreement ratified by the British parliament. His party was badly split on the issue and, after the general election of 1991, he only had a small parliamentary majority. Not until the summer of 1993, after a very difficult passage through parliament, did Britain finally agree to the Maastricht Treaty.

Meanwhile, German unification was causing many problems to the previously strong German economy, the health of which was further weakened by a worldwide recession. A severe currency crisis in the summer of 1993 was a great setback to the plans for a European monetary union.

The revolutions in Eastern Europe of 1989 and 1990 seemed to herald the dawn of a happy new age of greater freedom, peace, prosperity and co-operation from one end of Europe to the other but, very quickly, optimistic hopes faded. By 1993 the dark clouds of war, recession and uncertainty were closing in.

Source 3

The break up of Yugoslavia, January 1993. Protected by the fog from Serb and Croat snipers in the surrounding hills, a Bosnian Muslim woman prays beside the grave of a recently killed relative in the cemetery at Sarajevo.